Easy English for Simple Homeschooling

How to Teach, Assess, and Document High School English

Lee Binz,
The HomeScholar

© 2017 by **The HomeScholar LLC**

All Rights Reserved. No part of this publication may be reproduced in any form or by any means, including scanning, photocopying, or otherwise without prior written permission of the copyright holder.

First Printing, 2014

Printed in the United States of America

Cover Design by Robin Montoya
Edited by Kimberly Charron

ISBN: 1499385374
ISBN-13: 978-1499385373

Disclaimer: Parents assume full responsibility for the education of their children in accordance with state law. College requirements vary, so make sure to check with the colleges about specific requirements for homeschoolers. We offer no guarantees, written or implied, that the use of our products and services will result in college admissions or scholarship awards.

Easy English for Simple Homeschooling

How to Teach, Assess, and Document High School English

What are Coffee Break Books?

Easy English for Simple Homeschooling is part of The HomeScholar's Coffee Break Book series.

Designed especially for parents who don't want to spend hours and hours reading a 400-page book on homeschooling high school, each book combines Lee's practical and friendly approach with detailed, but easy-to-digest information, perfect to read over a cup of coffee at your favorite coffee shop!

Never overwhelming, always accessible and manageable, each book in the series will give parents the tools they need to tackle the tasks of homeschooling high school, one warm sip at a time.

Everything about these Coffee Break Books is designed to suggest simplicity, ease, and comfort—from the size (fits in a purse), to the font and paragraph length (easy on the eyes), to the price (the same as a Starbucks Venti Triple Caramel Macchiato). Unlike a fancy coffee drink, however, these books are guilt-free pleasures you will want to enjoy again and again!

Table of Contents

What are Coffee Break Books? v
A Giant Montage of Guilt 9
English in Plain English 13
Teaching Writing 19
Literary Analysis and Test Preparation 25
What is a Credit? 31
How to Determine Grades 35
Unique Learners 41
Homeschool Records..51
Curriculum Suggestions...................................65
Quick Essay Skills Earn Thanks.......................73
The HomeScholar's Reading List for the College Bound 83
Afterword...107
Who is Lee Binz, and What Can She Do for Me?107
Testimonials 109
Also From The HomeScholar.........................113

Introduction

A Giant Montage of Guilt

I had difficulty teaching English in my homeschool. High school English can be confusing. So many skills and topics can come under the heading of English, such as ... communication skills, spelling, grammar, vocabulary, punctuation, penmanship, composition, reports, poetry, prose, reading skills, reading for pleasure, classical literature, nonfiction, reading aloud, speed reading, comprehension, public speaking, speech and debate, American literature, British literature, great books, literary analysis, essay writing, timed essays, sentence structure, paragraph, outline, mythology, fables, capitalization, parts of speech, dialogue, word choice, editing, novel writing, short stories, lyrics, iambic pentameter, haiku, expository narrative, summary, creative writing, note taking, persuasive literature, bibliography, biography, themes, Shakespeare, irony, listening skills, character, setting, rhetoric, Socratic dialogue ... and the list goes on!

When I looked at high school English, it felt like a giant montage of guilt. I thought I should cover all of it—during the first month of 9th grade! It seemed overwhelming.

The first thing to recognize is that you can't possibly do everything, and you certainly can't do it all in one year. Focus on what is important in high school English: reading and writing.

How do you feel about teaching English? For me, it was a little scary, difficult to teach, and intimidating. Some parents think it takes thousands of hours with buckets of tears. For other parents, it is unending joy.

We can all agree it's important, because it builds life and work skills. These are important to develop to function in society. Our feelings about English may be mixed, but it's important.

Chapter 1

English in Plain English

A high school English class means working on communication skills. That's what you're teaching in English—communication. This means writing skills, including spelling, grammar, vocabulary, punctuation, penmanship, composition, reports, poetry, and prose.

English also includes work on reading skills, such as reading for fun, reading literature for school, nonfiction, poetry, parents reading aloud, speed-reading classes, and reading comprehension.

English can also include speaking skills such as public speaking, speech and debate, speaking at church, Toastmasters, or Teen Pact. These experiences can help make students more comfortable when they speak in front of groups.

In high school, not all kids continue with skills workbooks. For example, if they already spell reasonably well, instead of using Spelling Power, All About Spelling, *and* Sequential Spelling, maybe your child doesn't need to study spelling at all in high school. Instead of teaching a rigorous grammar curriculum every year, maybe you'll see that Winston Grammar is all your child needs. Your approach to vocabulary development may also change. You can use games and activities. See my article, "Play Your Way to a Great Vocabulary" at HomeHighSchoolHelp.com for some ideas. In addition, the card games Rummy Roots and More Rummy Roots can help build vocabulary skills.

Focus on what is important: reading and writing. There are many ways to get there, not everything needs to be covered by all children, and there are many paths to get where you need to go. So, relax!

What is Required?

When people talk about what's required for courses, it can be confusing, because there are two different kinds of requirements. There are high school graduation requirements (what your child needs to graduate), and there are college admission requirements (what your child needs to get into college).

For English, this is not an issue, because whether your goal is college admission or high school graduation, the requirements are the same. You simply have to provide four years of English during high school.

Provide one credit each year of high school. Teach your student reading at their level and writing at their level. By level, I mean ability level, not grade level.

How Much Each Year?

Usually one credit of English per year is all your child needs, all that is required, and all that I suggest. English is one credit, unless you happen to use two complete English programs, as written, in which case each English program is one credit. However, I usually don't recommend more than one.

I think it's always best to avoid overwork and not double up. When you double up in a subject area, it can cause burn out, not only for children, but also for parents. It's hard to keep up with.

If English is the subject your child struggles with, doing too much can cause even more burn out. It can kill the love of learning, and make your child feel stupid and incompetent, so they end up getting worse as a result.

If it's their weak area, I recommend keeping English to one credit per year. Don't try to get them up to grade level within one year of school, especially if it means two or three levels, because this can backfire. If it is their weak area, working on one credit per year is especially important.

The only exception to the one-credit-per-year guideline is if your child has special interests and wants to study more. When we homeschooled, my children loved reading. We planned out our curriculum with Sonlight, which includes writing and tons of reading. It is a pre-measured curriculum and English is one credit each year.

But my children also wanted to write a novel! They saw "Learn to Write the Novel Way" and wanted to use it. We worked on both Sonlight and the novel curriculum in one year. Honestly, this is one of the reasons I don't recommend it, because I thought I was going to die! It was the hardest year, ever! I think the only reason any of us survived at all is because the desire to do both courses came from my children.

For most kids, one credit of English per year is perfectly fine. Unless your child's interest is driving more than one (and even then, be careful), don't overload your child with more than one English curriculum per year.

Chapter 2

Teaching Writing

The most important English skills to teach are skills that will be used in college and in life. These include: speaking skills, reading skills, and writing skills.

Speaking skills can be improved through participation in any number of public speaking opportunities (see previous chapter). Reading skills can be improved through regular exposure to good writing, but teaching writing skills seems to intimidate many homeschool parents.

There are many reasons to teach writing skills. First, college admission tests include writing. The SAT and the ACT each offer a timed essay, and Advanced

Placement (AP) exams require them. They are essentially long essay tests.

Beyond testing, writing is also necessary for college application essays. Your child will have to sit down and write a paper about themselves or an experience they've had, turn it in to a college, and hope they will earn admission and scholarships.

Writing skills can also help with scholarship applications, because organizations often ask for essays about a certain topic or a student's goals.

Writing skills are important for life, job skills, living skills, home educating your own children, writing letters to the editor, or blogging.

Quick Essays

One specific kind of writing is used repeatedly in college and in life—the quick essay. When they had to write college admission essays, my children became overwhelmed with the thought that one or two essays would represent them to college admission officials.

To help them, I assigned a quick essay about a time they taught chess to a group. They wrote it out as a quick essay, and that was how I got it out of their heads. I found the skills developed from writing quick essays helped them with college application essays.

You can practice the quick essay by including timed essay writing each year. If you're preparing for the SAT or the ACT test, each includes an optional, timed essay.

Essays are required in real life, too. When you apply for a job, they often ask you to write a few paragraphs about yourself, and you only have a few minutes to do so.

We need to be able to write quickly as adults, too; I only set aside 30 minutes of my time to write my Christmas letter, which can be challenging!

The ability to write quick essays is important. It's one of those things students need to do repeatedly in college.

Not everything is a fill-in-the-bubble test; there are many times in college when a student is asked to write a quick essay. For instance, they may be asked to write a lab report or write tests with quick essays as a literature major in college.

Teaching my children how to write a quick essay was important when we were homeschooling, and they found it even more important when they went away to college. It was the most important aspect of English we taught at home.

You can use quick essays to document other classes, too. I did that quite often. One day a week, I had my children write a quick essay about what they were learning in history or art class, or any other subject we were studying.

It gave me a way to document and provide work samples for classes other than English, and was a great way to evaluate my children without using a test.

For example, in foreign language, they wrote a quick essay about a country which speaks French. That gave me a way to grade them without using a fill-in-the-bubble type test.

One of the reasons I'm careful to encourage parents to teach quick essay writing skills is because my children came back and thanked me for teaching them.

My son Alex hadn't been in college for a month when he came back home after his first essay class and said thank you.

To him, it was apparent that most of the people in the class had never taken an essay test before. He sat down, the professor handed him an essay prompt, and he simply completed it like a quick essay. Everybody in the class was frustrated and didn't know how to do it, while he was well prepared.

For more information about quick essays, see **Appendix 1: Quick Essay Skills Earn Thanks.**

Chapter 3

Literary Analysis and Test Preparation

Literary analysis is not a high school requirement. I thought great homeschools had to include Socratic dialog. After reading books, these mythical homeschoolers enjoy deep and rich conversations about the nuances of great works of literature. They share meaningful discussions about historical perspectives and relevant insights within classical and modern literature.

Meanwhile, I got comments such as, "Great book, mom … what's next?" I admire parents who include literary analysis, but I simply wasn't capable. I used a literature based curriculum, so it seems strange to say it, but I hate literary analysis. We preferred to read books all the time.

The truth is, I always felt guilty about not including literary analysis. Every homeschool mom has her one "thing" that keeps her awake at night, and literary analysis was a struggle for me. On tests and worksheets, my children seemed to have terrible reading comprehension, yet they were reading all the time. They read all day long and late into the night. They laughed and cried and gasped when they read silently to themselves. They begged me to continue when I read aloud to them. How could they do so poorly on reading comprehension questions when they seemed to understand while they were reading?

How do you know when you have succeeded in teaching your child English? When I was homeschooling, I was so stressed out about literary analysis. Every year, I spent a ridiculous amount of time looking at Progeny Press, Learning Language Arts Through Literature, and other curriculum. Why was I failing? Why couldn't I teach literary analysis? Every time I asked my kids, "How did you like the book?" I never got any insightful dialog about the deeper meaning of the literature.

I finally decided that my goal for literature would be the same as my goal for Bible study. My goal when teaching the Bible was for my kids to love their Bible, not analyze their Bible. Therefore, I taught them to love literature instead of analyze it. I didn't want to "beat the love of books out of them" by making them analyze everything.

In retrospect, it all ended up great. Ironically, they both ended up in a "Great Books" honors program, analyzing literature at a college level by their own choice! They were able to do college level literary analysis in their honors class without a problem, getting great grades. Their only frustration with the class was reading the occasional book synopsis. "I would rather read the whole thing – they miss the best parts!"

As one mother wrote,

> Honest, good, hard-working homeschooling moms are doing the right thing when they don't tear, claw, dissect, and shred books the children used to love. You know, I thought "classic" meant "boring" until I was about 30. Suddenly it struck me that "classic" means that thousands of avid readers made a list of books they loved and highly recommend.

I may have lost the literary analysis battle, but I won the war. I was stressed out when they were in high school, but I can honestly say that I achieved my goal: they love reading. Keeping the focus on "love of learning" is so difficult, though, when you are faced with a kid who may only answer "fine" when you ask them about their reading. Ultimately, it is the love of reading that matters.

Test Preparation

Regardless of whether you include literary analysis in your homeschooling, it can be helpful to work on test preparation for reading comprehension. Most standardized tests include reading comprehension, so if your child knows ahead of time how to answer questions about a passage of literature, they will be better prepared.

I knew that doing test preparation with my sons was not the same thing as either understanding or enjoying a book. Instead, it was figuring out what questions test writers were likely to ask about, and how to answer those questions, even when they were phrased in strange ways.

Studying with real SAT tests is the best way to do test preparation so you can see literature-based questions repeatedly. If your child practices, soon they will come to understand the typical comprehension questions they will see on the SAT or ACT.

Chapter 4

What is a Credit?

How do you determine an English credit? The guidelines are the same for all homeschool classes, not just English. High school credit can be based on the number of hours worked when the student is at high school age, or the content of a curriculum.

If you use one complete curriculum for English, you award one whole high school credit for that activity. But sometimes homeschoolers combine various curricula together, mixing a little bit of this and a little bit of that. For instance, you might combine a little bit of American literature with some British and Russian literature, in which case it's best to count hours.

When you count hours, one high school credit is equivalent to 120 to 180 hours of work. If your student works 60 to 90 hours, they have earned a half credit.

You don't have to painstakingly count every single hour, you can easily estimate those hours. If your student works an hour a day on a subject, that will typically add up to one high school credit. If they work half an hour a day, then they will earn half of a high school credit.

As I mentioned in Chapter 1, I usually recommend that students take only one high school English credit per year, to avoid the risk of burnout. But if your child does quite a bit of public speaking, is involved in speech and debate or Toast Masters, or does something that has them talking in front of people all the time, that could easily add up to 90 hours of a public speaking class, in which case they've earned half a credit.

In addition to this, you might still have a one-credit class on American literature. In that case, you use both methods of determining credit—counting hours and using a measured curriculum.

Including Skills and Estimating Hours

If you are estimating the number of hours your child spends on English, remember that the credit should include all the different English skills they practice. Include all of their writing and reading activities per week (including reading for fun or reading for school).

English includes a lot of different skills, so be sure to count them all towards that credit. Include the number of hours for instruction, practice, and work. If you count all these hours over the course of the school year, you'll probably have more than 180.

English is one of those skills that takes practice, much like math. When your student did 6th grade math, it probably only took half an hour to get the lesson done. By the time your child gets into high school math, such as Geometry or Pre-Calculus, it can take hours to get a whole lesson done. English is like that, too; it takes a lot of practice.

I like to provide nice, soft boundaries for determining English credit. It takes about 1 to 2 hours per day for an English credit, or about 5 to 10 hours per week, or about 150 hours per year.

Some homeschoolers I know do a lot of traveling, and may work on writing for only a few months out of the year. For them, it may make more sense to count 150 hours per year.

Others have the same schedule every single day. For them, estimating one or two hours per day is quite easy. If you spend one or two days in town, then three or four days on the farm doing work at home, etc. For you, it makes more sense to count the number of hours per week.

The point is to do what works and makes sense for your own family and methods. Don't obsess too much over the tiny details!

Chapter 5

How to Determine Grades

Determining grades for English can sometimes be challenging. English includes writing and reading; how do you grade writing and reading?!

Grading for English should include daily work, such as completion of assigned reading and writing.

How do you determine a grade for the day-to-day work? How do you determine a grade if you haven't been grading day-to-day? Estimating grades is one method you can use, whether for a single paper or a whole English class.

If you use mastery in your homeschool and your child meets your high expectations, you can give a grade of A or 4.0. In the same way, if your child has high test scores (perhaps from a standardized test or SAT test), you can give an A or a 4.0.

If your child loves a subject, chances are they will know more than is measured by a test, because they love the subject, which can also demonstrate A-level work.

You can give your child a B, or a 3.0, if they did well, but you feel confident they have not done A-level work.

You can give your child a C, or a 2.0, if their work wasn't good, but they kept going to the next level. They did enough to pass, and moved forward, but did not excel.

In my homeschool, I only used fill-in-the-bubble tests for about half of our classes. For the rest, I estimated my children's grades. My children thought those grades were bogus and even told me so! However, I know they were honest and true.

The "proof was in the pudding" as they say, when my children went to college. There, they discovered that when compared to their college professors, I was a hard grader!

Grouch-Free English Grading

Grouch-free English grading is possible! There is a difference between grading a paper and putting a grade on a transcript.

When you grade only one thing, you give one grade. When you put a final grade on a transcript, you should include the total of all the ways you have evaluated your student. This final grade needs to include all of the methods of evaluation you used.

Learning to write is a messy process. You start off with a rough draft, learn through practice, and get better with feedback. Your goal is to give your student practice with feedback. Once you've given them lots of feedback, then you can give them a final grade on their finished product.

It's a little like eating a sausage raw from the factory—you wouldn't do that! You would wait until it was cooked!

Combine all of the aspects of your child's English work—reading activities, writing activities, daily work of all kinds—for their final transcript grade. Everything you call English should be included.

You could base a third of your student's grade on the books they read, the instruction you gave, or the curriculum you used. Their writing could be a third of their grade—you could list all the things they wrote, such as reports, essays, journal writing, or blogging.

Their daily work could be one-third of the grade, too, including the day-to-day instruction, class participation, or workbooks they completed.

You could also divide it into thirds and call it reading, writing, and speaking. Or you could divide your grade into three even parts and call one-third "Analysis," one-third "Composition," and one-third "Assignments."

Whatever you decide, combine all of the different ways you evaluated into one final grade on the transcript.

Chapter 6

Unique Learners

Not everybody is at the center of the bell-shaped curve, and most children are unique learners.

When your children are outside the bell-shaped curve, whether they're struggling learners or gifted learners, your focus should remain the same. Your focus should be on learning reading and writing skills.

A high school age student earns high school credit when they're in high school. If your struggling learner was in a public high school, their classes would be on their high school transcript all the time, every single time, even if they were below grade level. Everything they did in school would be on their transcript. You can do this in your homeschool, too. High school age students earn high school credit, regardless of their "level."

All students need daily writing practice (even if they're already good writers), to maintain their skills and improve. They also need practice writing even if they struggle with it.

Encourage Reading

No matter which side of the bell-shaped curve your child is on, encourage them to read.

For some reluctant students, it's helpful to look for reading material in their area of specialization. Some students are more likely to read books about their passions.

My son Kevin read a staggering number of books on chess. It's what he loved, and what he read about.

Instead of books, your child may love to read magazines or trade journals. My other son, Alex, hung out with many kids who loved economics. They spent a lot of time reading *Rich Dad, Poor Dad*, "Money Magazine," and "Entrepreneur."

Think about what your child loves, and find them books or other reading material that will capture their interest.

Reluctant Readers

If you have a reluctant reader, it's important to remember that you are not alone. I talk to plenty of parents who have reluctant readers, and there are many ways to encourage these students to spend more time reading.

First, try to include high quality books. With reluctant readers, sometimes we mistakenly use a curriculum with books written for the English curriculum, and often these books aren't high quality literature. Consider higher quality literature and don't be afraid to use books that are below their grade or reading level, which will encourage them toward success.

The more successful they are in reading, the faster your child will get and the more they'll enjoy it. They will get better when you provide easier books for them to read, especially if these books are high quality, real literature books.

Another way to encourage a reluctant reader is to focus on reading during the summer when they have a bit more time. Consider reading aloud the first two chapters of a book, and then let them continue from there. You will be amazed at how this will help!

Getting started can sometimes be the hardest part for reluctant readers. They don't understand the characters, and can be frustrated by some of the vocabulary. When you start by reading a book aloud to them, they'll get more involved and may be eager to continue.

Mixing in some audio books is a great way to encourage your slow reader. Make sure your child can read from a text, of course, but supplementing with audio is a great way to encourage them.

You can mix in audio books for some of the great literature you use, which is a good way to help them with books above their grade level.

Have them read other books at or below grade level from a traditional text, to keep them practicing. This is a great way to expand their reading list.

There are many short classics accessible to slow readers. For example, have your child read *Call of the Wild*, which is quite short, rather than *The Last of the Mohicans*, which is quite long.

Or they could read *The Red Badge of Courage*, a war novel, rather than *War and Peace*, which is world-renowned as one of the longest (and dare I say most boring?!) books on the classics list.

They could read *The Old Man and the Sea*, which is a short book about an old man's adventure at sea, instead of *Moby Dick*, which is a huge book.

There are ways you can fill in with short, classic books. Instead of reading more overwhelming books that could take a reluctant reader six months to get through, read *Call of the Wild*, which might only take three or four weeks to get through.

If you need some suggestions for your reluctant reader, look at my **Reading List for the College Bound** in Appendix 2.

Active Learners

If you have an active learner, one who might be a good reader but is always out doing or moving, it can be helpful to find books with active main characters.

For example, encourage an active child to read books about Tom Sawyer, who is a very active, mischievous character, rather than books by Jane Austin, who writes from a feelings perspective.

Another way to encourage these readers is to give them books in the same genre as the movies they enjoy. If they like science fiction, try to find classic science fiction books.

Nonfiction is fine, too. If they want to read books about Tony Hawke or *How to Be a Better Skier*, they can go ahead. If you get stuck on what to choose, you can always ask the librarian.

Another way to encourage both active and struggling learners is to watch the stage play of a book you're reading. It could be Shakespeare or "Death of a Salesman," but watching the play at the same time makes it go much faster, and keeps active and struggling readers from getting frustrated.

If you are reading a Shakespeare play, you could also watch or listen to the play at the BBC online. This is helpful for active learners, because the book can make more sense to them when they see it acted out. With something like Shakespeare, where the vocabulary is a little antiquated, it can be hard to follow along if they don't have an extensive vocabulary.

Grade Level English

Some parents get anxious about making sure their child is at grade level in English, but when your goal is to teach them something new and to practice until it becomes easier for them, everyone wins.

Practice with success is where you see the most improvement. If you ask your child to do something they cannot possibly do, they will have increasingly more trouble with it. Eventually, they may lose their confidence and ability to read or write. They might lose the love of learning, and may end up hating reading and writing.

It's better to be below grade level and learn than to be at grade level and be unsuccessful and fail. This is something that Andrew Pudewa of the Institute for Excellence in Writing talks about. He says it's better to have children practice at something they *can* do so they'll get better, rather than asking them to do something they can't possibly do, because they're not ready for it and can end up getting worse.

Andrew and I had a conversation about grade level English. He said you can't define what a 10th grade writing standard is. When you look at public school requirements, they're so vague that it's almost meaningless to somebody looking for a concrete definition of what grade level English is.

It's so vague that you can't define it. Even teachers in public schools have the flexibility to provide what is needed for a child to succeed. If a student is working at a 4th grade writing level but is in 10th grade, the teacher won't constantly give them assignments above their ability level.

If the concept of "grade level writing" still has you stressed out, here's a story of my son's experience in college. When they started college, both my sons were shocked at the low skill levels of some of the students. As homeschoolers, we're not used to seeing the huge variation in skills more common in public high schools.

When my children were in community college, they had to do a peer review of another student's writing, and were quite shocked at how poorly students wrote in College English 101.

Later, after graduation, my younger son tutored students in writing skills. He was shocked to learn that the 10th grade student he was tutoring wrote at a 4th grade ability level, but was earning A's and high school credit in his public school English class.

I'm not encouraging you to adopt a low standard; I simply want to encourage you not to become overly concerned about the concept of grade level in writing. Keep moving forward with your child and helping them do the next thing, and they will continue to improve.

Chapter 7

Homeschool Records

After you've determined which English courses your child will take and what methods you will use to grade them, the next important task is to record their learning.

When you create your transcript, be specific for class titles. Avoid broad class titles such as "English 9" or "Language Arts." The titles I tend to default to for English are "Grammar and Composition" or "Literature and Composition."

"Literature and Composition" is my favorite, because when you break this phrase down, you will see that literature means reading and composition means writing. Literature and composition literally mean reading and writing, which almost everybody covers.

If you use a curriculum specific to grammar, such as "Easy Grammar," it might be a good idea to call your class "Grammar and Composition." Look at the title of the curriculum you use, and see if your curriculum will give you some tips about the name of your class. You could use the title "Novel Writing" if you use "Learn to Write the Novel Way" or the "One-Year Novel Adventure" series. If you emphasized American authors, then consider "American Literature and Composition."

It's okay to have unusual classes for English as well. My brother-in-law taught English classes at a local public high school, and taught a class called "Sports Communication." The speech component of this course included learning how to do a baseball play-by-play analysis. The students listened to a baseball game and wrote a newspaper column afterward! (My niece was in the class, so my brother-in-law taught his own daughter in his public high school class!)

We feel as if our grades are subjective, I'm sure that's true all the time anyway, but don't hesitate to evaluate your own children. (It even happens in public school sometimes!) If you get stuck, I suggest a class title of "Literature and Composition."

Honors English

How do you know whether your English class is an honors class? The word "honors" is extremely subjective, and can mean anything you want it to mean. It means more than high school level, or, in other words, college level work.

If you're confident your child is doing college level work, you might call their course "Honors English." An easy way to know your child is working at the college level is to have them take an AP or CLEP test, which shows a college level learning ability.

If they take a college class at your local community college (or dual enrollment), or an online college course, they all demonstrate college level skills.

Remember that English always takes plenty of time each day—probably more than an hour. Simply because you work for two hours on English every day doesn't mean that it needs to be an honors class. Just as when you get to upper level math, English takes more than an hour a day when you get into the high school levels.

Weighting Classes

If you are going to provide an "Honors" designation on your child's transcript, then you might think about whether you should weight your student's grades. Weighting has nothing to do with your bathroom scale. A grade of A in a class usually equals a numerical grade of 4.0. For an honors class, some schools will weight an A as a 5.0, and some schools will weight it as a 4.5.

When you weight credits, a regular class credit equals 1.0 for the whole class. But for an honors class, some schools award a weighted credit of 2.0 or 1.5.

Interestingly, all the high schools across the United States weight their classes differently. However, colleges know this. They know that all schools weight classes differently, so the first thing they do when they see weighted grades is to "unweight" them, and put them all back to 4.0 and 1.0, and then re-weight them according to their own system.

Colleges might consider some of your classes honors, and give more weight to them, or may not consider AP Art an honors class and won't weight it. They will "unweight" and then "re-weight" based on their own criterion, which is why I do not suggest you weight your classes, even if you include honors classes.

The only exception is when a college requests you weight grades on the application. Otherwise, I think it's difficult for parents; it's harder to do the math, it's a bit more frustrating, and it's hard to maintain consistency across all of your classes. I don't think it's useful, so I don't usually recommend it.

Course Descriptions

Whether your child's class is an honors class or a normal class, course descriptions are helpful—they are recommended.

Create course descriptions that describe your class, the curriculum you used, a description of how you graded, and the books your child read. When you use a literature based curriculum, the boundaries between English course descriptions, history course descriptions, and reading lists get blurry! Instead of thinking you need to divide books between them all, think of it like a Venn diagram.

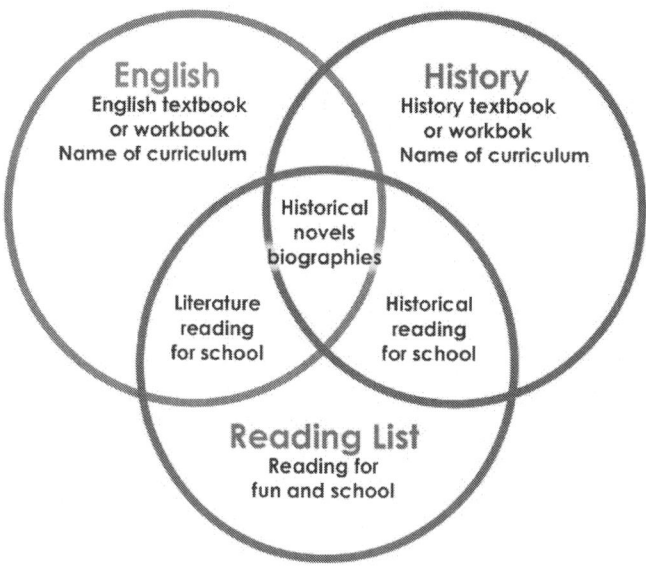

Books to add only in the English course description include textbooks, workbooks, and curriculum, such as Sonlight Core 100, Spelling Power, Wordly Wise, or Institute for Excellence in Writing High School Essay Intensive. In the history course description, include textbooks, workbooks, and curriculum, such as Sonlight Core 100, Mapping the World By Heart, or A History of US by Joy Hakim.

And there are books that go in both the English course description and the reading list, such as literature read for school. For example, The Red Badge of Courage, or The Call of the Wild. There are books that go in both the history course description and the reading list, such as biographies and historical fiction read for school. For example: Autobiography of Benjamin Franklin or Farewell to Manzanar. If books fit in both the history course description and the English course description, I would put the autobiographies in history and the historical novels in English, even though they help the child learn about both subjects.

Because homeschoolers who use a literature based curriculum have so many books in the reading list (and always will, no doubt), I'd be tempted to remove the more schoolish books (such as Famous Men of Greece) and put them only in the course description, rather than on the reading list. But you know, this is only a preference. Most public high school kids read 5 to 10 books a year, so there is no need to include everything, and these completely overlap! Although my son, Alex, read

Jane Austen's books for fun and should have had those books on his reading list, the same books were also on Kevin's reading list, even though he didn't think it was much fun at all!

The grading criteria part of the course description could include what your child read and wrote, and the mechanics of English. When describing what they wrote, include essay titles, such as: An Essay on the Civil War or An Essay on World War II. Or you could include the <u>kinds</u> of writing they worked on, such as quick essay, research report, short story, or poetry.

List what they did, such as workbooks or the skills you taught, such as punctuation, grammar, and spelling.

List the classes they attended, curriculum used, or how they tested.

You may choose to base part of their grade on the mechanics of English, which could include vocabulary, comprehension, spelling, and expression. These words are from an

Iowa Test of Basic Skills that my sons took; I counted the English portion of this assessment as part of their course description and grades. My children scored above average in those areas on the assessment, so I gave them 100% for each of the areas on the test.

Reading List

Another important item to include in your record keeping is a reading list. A reading list is not a bibliography. Simply include title and author. Your child's reading list can include books read for school, for work, and for pleasure.

You can include classic literature, historical reading, popular novels, biographies, and any reading for fun. I usually exclude anything that seems like curriculum. Anthologies are collections of literature excerpts, and can be a little harder to place. When a reading list is already quite long, I suggest leaving the anthology as curriculum, either in the English course description or the history course description (or both!) but not on the reading list.

I did include an unending list of economics books on my youngest son's list, and tons of chess books on my eldest son's list.

The goal of a reading list is to include somewhere between 6 and 600 books per year. If you have a reluctant reader, strive for 6. The list will still be impressive. Some schools can't get 6 books into their kids. If you have a reluctant reader, try to include audio books, books made into movies, or plays.

For prolific readers, you don't need 600 books on your list; once you get 40 to 50 books on the list, that's enough! This will indicate that your child is a prolific reader.

Overlapping Subject Areas

When you think about reading lists, course descriptions, and class titles, one of the first things you'll notice is a huge overlap in subject areas.

Books can be used in overlapping areas. Sometimes a single book might be considered English, but it could also be history and be on the reading list. What do you do?

I usually suggest including any textbooks, workbooks, or names of curriculum on your child's English course description, and include anything you assigned for school, or any literature they read for fun. The English course description would include historical novels, biographies, or autobiographies which come from history.

This is literature, but it's also history, and it can go on your English class course description. These overlapping areas might be English, social studies, and the reading list, and you can include the texts in more than one course description.

This happens in schools all the time. It's called integrated curriculum or writing across the curriculum. It's extremely popular in public schools right now;

homeschoolers have been doing this for years.

We're trying to get that two for one; it's perfectly fine for you to include books in multiple course descriptions if you want to.

Chapter 8

Curriculum Suggestions

Parents often ask me for curriculum suggestions, and to be quite honest, I feel uncomfortable making recommendations.

Curriculum choices vary based on the learning style of the student. I can tell you which curriculum is nationally ranked, well received by many homeschoolers, or highly reviewed, but this doesn't mean it will be a good fit for your child.

However, there are certain curriculum I think are wonderful, and they are the ones I usually suggest parents look at first, and then look beyond them if they need to. The Institute for Excellence in Writing (www.IEW.com) offers some wonderful writing and literature programs. I used the Advanced Communication series when my children were in 11th grade. That was how they learned to write a quick essay. I watched the entire Student Essay Intensive from IEW and it was wonderful. Their programs are excellent.

Write Shop (www.WriteShop.com) is also a good program. They offer online support, excellent writing prompts, and everything is easy to use.

Brave Writer (www.BraveWriter.com) is a curriculum many of my Gold Care Club members love. The heart of Brave Writer is a reverence for unique writing voice (from pre-readers to adulthood) and encouraging the unique style of the writer through gentle care, adequate support, and kind alliance of a parent.

They come alongside the parent with a robust online classroom and manuals, encouraging growth in both children writers and parent writing coaches, so the relationship between homeschooling parent and child is nurtured.

Two more good English curriculum choices are WriteAtHome (WriteatHome.com) and Home2Teach (Home2Teach.com). Or you could consider a literature based curriculum that blends English and history together.

Sonlight (www.Sonlight.com) language arts is what I used through 10th grade. We used Sonlight for writing, from the time we started homeschooling in 3rd and 5th grade up until 10th grade. We absolutely loved it and it was extremely helpful. I think it was all because of the practice, practice, practice.

In addition to Sonlight, consider another literature based curriculum:

- Tapestry of Grace
- My Father's World
- The Well-Trained Mind
- Robinson Curriculum
- Beautiful Feet Books
- Veritas Press
- Truth Quest History
- Notgrass History

- The Noah Plan
- AmblesideOnline
- BookShark

If you buy a curriculum that focuses on reading, remember to include writing. If you buy a curriculum that focuses on writing, remember to include some books. Your homeschool English class should include both. But be careful not to overwork your child using multiple programs, unless it's something your child loves and wants to do.

Beyond a standard curriculum, you could use a delight directed approach with Learn to Write the Novel Way. Or branch out with fun topics such as a year of poetry study, memorization, and writing. You can focus on English skills needed for the SAT essay by using writing prompts found in Cracking the AP English Language & Composition Exam by Princeton Review. Or, your child can learn essay skills that will help them apply for scholarships, so you can defray the cost of college. I teach this concept in "College Scholarships for High School Credit" (Online Training) available on my website. If you focus on reading, perhaps your child merely needs daily writing practice, using the book, 501 Writing Prompts.

When you consider curriculum, here's the most important consideration. Your child's ability to write is what will earn them scholarship money when they apply to college.

If somebody were to pay you $40,000 in cash to write an essay, you would probably do it. And if you knew your child would get $40,000 in cash for writing an essay, you would probably buy a $100 curriculum. As expensive as English curriculum can seem, try to think about it in the grand scheme of things.

The English curriculum you buy can earn your child good scholarships, can help them get a job, and help them advance.

You can't find a better place to spend $100 on curriculum than English, because it can save a ton of money in the long run.

Focus on What's Important

Teaching English in high school is easy if you keep your focus on what is important—encouraging your child to love books and write competently. Of these two goals, the first, in my opinion, is the most important. A passion for reading will stay with a child through college and into adulthood. In addition, someone who loves literature—especially excellent literature—will learn to write better naturally, simply by having the voice of the author in their head.

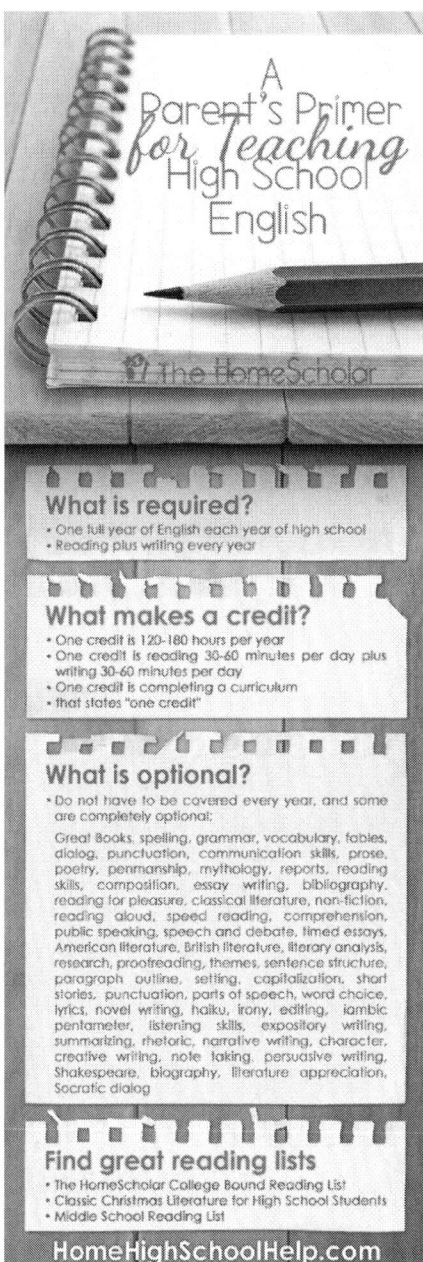

Appendix 1

Quick Essay Skills Earn Thanks

Thanks Mom!

What would you give to hear these words? "Thanks, Mom!" During Alex's first week at college, he thanked me for a skill I taught him when we were homeschooling. Believe it or not, he thanked me for teaching him how to write a quick essay.

A week into his transition at the university, his professor gave an essay test. Alex said the other students were somewhat freaked out by the all-essay format of the two-hour test. Because we had so carefully prepared our students to write a short essay under a high-pressure situation, Alex said he wasn't bothered by the test at all. He did recognize, however, that it was only because we had worked on the skill when he was homeschooling.

Learning to write a quick essay is an important part of college preparation for two reasons. Alex picked up on reason number one—colleges often give essay tests. The second reason for practicing quick essay skills is a little more immediate for homeschoolers. Your child needs the skill to score well on the SAT and ACT tests. Both tests contain a short essay. For both the SAT and ACT, the essay is optional, but certain colleges require the "optional essay."

Many colleges rely on SAT and ACT test scores to indicate college readiness. The writing section of these tests can provide outside documentation from a third party, demonstrating your child's ability to write. Test scores can determine the quality of college that will accept a student. In addition, universities frequently tie financial aid to test scores, giving an additional financial incentive to studying. Studying for these college admission tests, and learning how to write the essay required, can improve your child's chances of earning college admission and scholarships.

The SAT essay is 50 minutes long. It's a hand-written essay on a piece of paper, completed during a timed section of the exam. The essay is scanned into a computer and is visible to the college admission office, if they choose to view the essay online. You can see your child's essay online as well, which can be useful.

Handwriting is important, but not because of penmanship. The essay simply needs to be legible as well as written quickly. There is no specific style of penmanship required. By the time children reach high school, they have usually developed their own penmanship style, and that's fine.

How to Write a Short Essay

I would love to be able to tell you that I taught my children to write a short essay, but I didn't teach them. I did make sure they learned the skill, but I didn't do the teaching. I felt incompetent and unable to teach such a subjective skill as writing. How ironic, since I write for a living now! I didn't teach writing because I didn't feel qualified, but I have heard from other parents that they couldn't teach writing because their children were resistant to parental instruction. Instead of worrying about who will teach what, focus on how to encourage your child to learn the necessary skill.

I delegated. We used a video tutorial that explained what was required so I didn't have to teach. I bought a book that provided writing prompts so I didn't have to have discussions about what an appropriate writing prompt would be. I paid for a visual example of corrected essays, so I could see for myself what a quality essay looked like. Once your child can write reasonably well, delegating to a self-teaching method of instruction can prepare your children very well.

My first purchase was the Institute for Excellence in Writing product called the Advanced Communication Series. This product is different than most IEW resources because it is a tutorial for the student, not for the parent. In other words, I didn't have to do anything with it other than make sure my children watched the video. The Advanced Communication Series teaches three distinct skills: taking notes from a college lecture, writing a long and short essay, and public speaking. Each section was wonderful, but the one I relied on most was the instruction in writing a short essay. After watching the video, we were ready for the children to try their new skills.

The book *501 Writing Prompts* by Learning Express is an inexpensive book filled with perfect prompts for short essays. Not surprisingly, the book contains 501 of these prompts! Beyond prompts, though, it provides some guidance for evaluating essays. It provides a scoring guide; the fancy word for that is "rubric." I hate the word rubric. When I pulled my children out of public school, the teacher said, "You don't even know what a rubric is?!" Ever since then I've hated the word! If you're like me, and rubric is Russian for "Pulling my hair out" then the book has the perfect help for you.

501 Writing Prompts includes model essays once every 25 prompts or so. The samples show you a top essay, a middle-of-the road essay, and a low-scoring essay. You can look at these sample essays and see how your student's writing compares. No rubric needed.

Look through the writing prompts book to find an appropriate essay. Because this book was intended for the general population, it does include "edgy" prompts that may not be appropriate for some homeschool families, so be sure to read each prompt first. If you prefer a book that can be used for a wider age range, look at the book *Writing Down the Days* by Lorraine M. Dahlstrom. I found it a little more difficult to adapt to a high school essay, but it does include prompts that are appropriate for all ages. Once you decide on a prompt, have your child write the essay using skills they learned from the IEW Advanced Communication Series.

Our homeschool wasn't all a bed of roses. It was very difficult for me to find the time to grade these essays by comparing them to the samples, and I got bogged down. Thankfully, my husband offered to step in and do the English grading for me. I felt terrible about having him do this, because I thought it was "my job" and I knew I was capable of it. Still, when he took over the grading, it was an enormous relief for me.

It wasn't all fun-and-games with my children, either. I remember how difficult the concept of timing was for my children. Kevin started the year by spending his first few minutes of each essay talking about how it wasn't possible to write an essay in such a short time. "I understand it's challenging, but you have 24 minutes left," I replied. After about 3 or 4 minutes of complaining, he figured out the clock was still ticking, and he would get busy.

We worked aggressively on essay writing using this strategy for sophomore year and junior year. I wanted to prepare my children for college, and I was very concerned about the SAT essay.

Practice Makes Perfect

Once you have identified instruction that works, and prompts that will help you use the instruction, you are half-way there. The most important key to a short essay is practice. We practiced short essay writing three times a week. I timed each essay for the same amount of time they are allowed for the SAT handwritten essay. When you think about it, 50 minutes three times a week isn't a huge time commitment. And from a parent's point of view, it's a great time of day. The kids are quietly scribbling away on paper while you can get the dishes or laundry done! It's a win-win for everyone!

We didn't always use prompts from *501 Writing Prompts* exactly as they were written. Sometimes I used prompts from real SAT tests. I found them in the book

10 Practice Tests for the SAT by Princeton Review. Each practice test included a prompt for the SAT essay, which was perfect practice for the test.

Sometimes I created my own prompt from our other homeschool subjects. At times, I used essay topics provided by our history curriculum or from other subjects. If a topic from the writing prompts book reminded me of a different subject, I would tweak it a bit to obtain an essay that fit what we were studying.

When my children were done with the essay, it provided written material for these classes that I could include in their course descriptions. It provided a way for me to "evaluate" my children in different subjects when I didn't use tests. It was great documentation for hard-to-document subjects.

Real success with learning to write a quick essay comes with practice. Once children learn how to write reasonably well, most additional success will come through practice.

Appendix 2

The HomeScholar's Reading List for the College Bound

The following selection of books is drawn from a variety of different reading lists, and represent the books that we at The HomeScholar are both familiar with and feel comfortable recommending to college-bound students.

It's not possible (or even desirable!) for any student to read all the books on every college-bound reading list, and not every book will be appropriate for every child. However, reading from a broad cross-section of both American and World literature will help prepare your students to understand a variety of different cultures and times, and strengthen their knowledge and understanding of great literature. We hope you enjoy this selection!

American Literature

Angelou, Maya *I Know Why the Caged Bird Sings*
Two children are abandoned by their mother and sent to live with their devout, self-sufficient grandmother in a small Southern town.

Cooper, James Fenimore *The Deerslayer*
A young white hunter brought up in the Delaware Indian tribe, must defend settlers before returning to the Iroquois who have allowed him parole.

Cooper, James Fenimore *Last of the Mohicans*
The story of the adopted son of the Mohicans, and the daughter of a British colonel, during the French and Indian War.

Crane, Stephen *The Red Badge of Courage*
A teenager enlists with the Union Army during the Civil War in the hopes of fulfilling his dreams of glory.

Fitzgerald, F. Scott *The Great Gatsby*
A portrait of the 1920s in America, this is the story of money, greed, excess, and a man in love.

Frank, Pat *Alas, Babylon*
A survival story that takes place after a nuclear attack destroys all civilization except for a small Florida town.

Franklin, Benjamin *The Autobiography of Benjamin Franklin*
Written initially to guide his son, Franklin's autobiography is a lively, spellbinding account of his unique and eventful life.

Haley, Alex *Roots*
This book chronicles several generations of a slave family, from a West African youth captured by slave raiders and

shipped to America in the 1700s, and concluding with the Civil War.

Hawthorne, Nathaniel *The Scarlet Letter*
Set in Puritan Boston, this book tells the story of a woman who conceives a daughter through an adulterous affair and struggles to create a new life of dignity and repentance.

Hemingway, Ernest *A Farewell to Arms*
The life of an American soldier and a British nurse against the backdrop of the First World War, cynical soldiers, fighting and the displacement of populations.

Keller, Helen *The Story of My Life*
A young woman overcomes the challenges of being both deaf and blind, with the help of her devoted teacher, Anne Sullivan.

Kennedy, John F. *Profiles in Courage*
John F. Kennedy profiles eight of his historical colleagues for their acts of astounding integrity in the face of overwhelming opposition.

Lee, Harper *To Kill a Mockingbird*
Exploration of civil rights and racism in the segregated southern United States of the 1930s.

Lewis, Sinclair *Main Street*
The story of a sophisticated young woman who moves to a small town in the American Midwest in 1912 and struggles against the small-minded culture of the citizens who live there.

London, Jack *Call of the Wild*
In the 19th-century Klondike Gold Rush, a domesticated dog is snatched and sold into a brutal life as a sled dog.

Malcom X, with Alex Haley *The Autobiography of Malcom X*
A narrative of spiritual conversion that outlines a controversial Black Muslim's philosophy of black pride, black nationalism, and pan-Africanism.

Miller, Arthur *Death of a Salesman*
An introspective dramatic play concerning the expectations we have for our lives, our failings and our inability to

find satisfaction with our place in the world.

Melville, Herman *Moby Dick*
The adventures of a wandering sailor and his voyage on a whale ship commanded by Captain Ahab, whose one purpose is to seek out a great white whale.

Paine, Thomas *Common Sense*
Paine's daring prose paved the way for the Declaration of Independence and the Revolutionary War.

Poe, Edgar Allan *Great Tales and Poems*
Stories and poems from one of the most famous creators of detective stories and supernatural tales.

Potok, Chaim *The Chosen*
Traces the friendship between two Jewish boys growing up in Brooklyn at the end of World War II.

Sinclair, Upton *The Jungle*
Explores the working man's lot at the turn of the century: the backbreaking

labor, the injustices of "wage-slavery," the bewildering chaos of urban life.

Steinbeck, John *The Grapes of Wrath*
This is the tale of a poor family of tenant farmers driven from their Oklahoma home by drought, economic hardship, and the Great Depression.

Stowe, Harriet Beecher *Uncle Tom's Cabin*
A slave whose child is to be sold, escapes her beloved home on a plantation in Kentucky and heads North, avoiding hired slave catchers, aided by the underground railroad.

Twain, Mark *The Adventures of Huckleberry Finn*
Huck Finn and his old friend Jim journey down the Mississippi river together.

Twain, Mark *The Adventures of Tom Sawyer*
A humorous and nostalgic book depicting the carefree days of boyhood in a small Midwestern town during the mid-1800s.

Twain, Mark *Innocents Abroad*
An acerbic account of the author's travels in Europe and the Near East, humorously describing both the places he visited and his fellow passengers on the voyage.

Walker, Alice *The Color Purple*
The story of two African-American sisters, a missionary in Africa, and a child-wife living in the South, told through their letters to each other.

Washington, Booker T. *Up From Slavery*
Autobiography of an influential spokesman and former slave, who became a major figure in the struggle for equal rights.

Wilder, Thornton *Our Town*
A study of life, love, and death in a New England town at the turn of the 20th century.

World Literature

Austen, Jane *Pride and Prejudice*
English country life is described in this much-loved English romance novel set in a society obsessed with profitable marriage contracts.

Austen, Jane *Sense and Sensibility*
This tale of manners and courtship in the 19th-century English countryside follows two sisters; one sensible, and the other impetuous.

Bronte, Charlotte *Jane Eyre*
In this romance and suspense novel, the orphaned governess Jane Eyre has a brooding, moody, wealthy employer with a terrible secret.

Bronte, Emily *Wuthering Heights*
A masterpiece of English romanticism, tells the story of love and revenge.

Carroll, Lewis *Alice's Adventures in Wonderland*
A fantasy about young Alice, who follows a white rabbit down a rabbit hole.

Cervantes, Miguel de *Don Quixote*
An eccentric old gentleman from La Mancha convinces himself that he is a knight. With his portly peasant squire, he sets out "tilting at windmills" to right the wrongs of the world.

Conrad, Joseph *Heart of Darkness*
Recounts a journey into the Congo and reveals the extent to which greed can corrupt a good man.

Defoe, Daniel *Robinson Crusoe*
An English sailor is marooned on a desert island for nearly three decades. He struggles to survive in extraordinary circumstances, and wrestles with fate and the nature of God.

Dickens, Charles *Great Expectations*
Traces the development of Pip from a boy of shallow aspirations to a man of depth and character.

Dickens, Charles *David Copperfield*
David Copperfield lives through trials and tribulations, first at a boys' school and then as a young man in London

before he goes to live with his great-aunt and eventually finds happiness.

Dickens, Charles *Tale of Two Cities*
Set during the French Revolution in the cities of Paris and London, a French aristocrat is accused of spying.

Dostoyevsky, Fyodor *The Gambler*
At a casino in Germany, a Russian family awaits news that a wealthy relative has died, but to their dismay, she arrives and begins gambling away their inheritance.

Dostoevsky, Fyodor *Crime and Punishment*
A poverty-stricken young man is faced with an opportunity to solve his financial problems with one simple but horrifying act: the murder of a pawnbroker.

Frank, Anne *The Diary of a Young Girl*
Traces the life of the Jewish girl who hid with seven other people in an attic for two years in Nazi-occupied Holland, and chronicles her day-to-day life in a diary.

Golding, William *Lord of the Flies*
A group of schoolboys stranded on an island soon revert to the state of primitive man, and engage in a struggle between savagery and civilization.

Hamilton, Edith *Mythology*
Discover the thrilling, enchanting, and fascinating world of Western mythology, from Odysseus's adventure-filled journey to the Norse god Odin's effort to postpone the final day of doom.

Homer *The Iliad*
An epic poem about Achilles' vengeance against Agamemnon and the city of Troy at the end of the Trojan War.

Homer *The Odyssey*
The story of Odysseus' difficulties in returning home after the Trojan War, which was won by the Greeks.

Huxley, Aldous *Brave New World*
This futuristic novel warns of the dangers of sacrificing freedom and individuality for scientific progress and social stability.

Kafka, Franz *Metamorphosis*
A seemingly typical man wakes up one morning to discover he has been transformed into a gigantic insect.

L'Engle, Madeleine *A Wrinkle in Time*
The story of friends on a dangerous and fantastic journey that will threaten their lives and our universe.

Lewis, C.S. *The Screwtape Letters*
This satirical piece portrays human life from the vantage point of Screwtape, and his correspondence with a novice demon in charge of the damnation of an ordinary young man.

Machiavelli, Niccolo *The Prince*
The world's most famous master plan for seizing and holding power. A disturbingly realistic and prophetic work on what it takes to be a prince...a king...a president.

Marlowe, Christopher *Doctor Faustus*
A well-respected German scholar grows dissatisfied with the limits of traditional forms of knowledge—logic, medicine,

law, and religion—and decides that he wants to learn to practice magic.

Milton, John *Paradise Lost*
Often considered the greatest epic in any modern language, this is the story of the revolt of Satan, his banishment from Heaven, and the fall of man and his expulsion from Eden.

Orwell, George *Animal Farm*
Domesticated animals stage a revolt against their cruel master. They soon find they have succeeded in exchanging one form of tyranny for another.

Plato *The Republic*
A monumental work of moral and political philosophy, presented as a dialogue between Socrates and others discussing the notion of a perfect community and the ideal individuals within it.

Remarque, Erich Maria *All Quiet on the Western Front*
Through the eyes and mind of a German private, the reader shares life on the battlefield during World War I.

Scott, Sir Walter *Ivanhoe*
Returning from fighting in the Crusades, the young Saxon knight Ivanhoe must fight to regain the woman he loves and to protect the social order and monarchy of England.

Shelley, Mary W. *Frankenstein*
Tampering with life and death, Dr. Frankenstein pieces together salvaged body parts to create a human monster.

Shakespeare, William *Romeo and Juliet*
The tale of two young star-crossed lovers and their families, who are caught in a destructive web of hatred.

Shakespeare, William *Twelfth Night*
After a shipwreck, twin siblings Viola and Sebastian wash up on the shores of Illyria. A story of mistaken identity and love entanglements.

Solzhenitsyn, Alexander *One Day in the Life of Ivan Denisovich*
This novel describes the oppression of totalitarian regimes, and the terrors of Stalin's prison camps.

Sophocles *Antigone*
Antigone defies her uncle, the new ruler, which starts a conflict between young and old, woman and man, individual and ruler, family and state.

Stevenson, Robert Louis *The Strange Case of Dr. Jekyll and Mr. Hyde*
Dr. Jekyll wants to rid his soul of evil, and in doing so creates the monstrous alter ego Mr. Hyde.

Swift, Jonathan *Gulliver's Travels*
Biting satire of British and European society, it follows a shipwrecked castaway encountering fantastical lands and creatures, including the petty, diminutive Lilliputians.

Tocqueville, Alexis de *Democracy in America*
Covering America's call for a free press to its embrace of the capitalist system, this book enlightens, entertains, and endures as a brilliant study of our national government and character.

Tolstoy, Leo *Anna Karenina*
Set against the backdrop of Moscow and St. Petersburg high society in the latter half of the nineteenth century, a woman forsakes her husband for a dashing count and brief happiness.

Tolkien, J.R.R *The Hobbit*
Bilbo Baggins, a respectable, well-to-do hobbit, lives comfortably in his hobbit-hole until the day the wandering wizard Gandalf chooses him to share in an adventure from which he may never return.

Tolstoy, Leo *War and Peace*
Tracks the evolution of five aristocratic families during the Napoleonic wars.

Wells, H.G. *The Time Machine*
A time traveler steps out of his time-transport machine in the year 802,700 to find Earth populated by a race of people supported by a slave class.

Wells, H.G. *War of the Worlds*
The first modern tale of alien invasion, this is a story of tentacled Martians attacking the Earth.

Wilde, Oscar *The Importance of Being Earnest*
This is a play about two men who bend the truth in order to add excitement to their lives.

Reluctant Readers

Your goal is to have your child read 6 to 60 books per year. For reluctant readers, reading the minimum number of books can be a challenge. Allow books below their reading level, so they increase their speed and fluency and gain confidence. Consider reading the first chapter aloud to get them interested in the story and understanding how to pronounce the character names before starting to read the book independently.

You want them to read at least 6 books a year with their own eyeballs, but mix in some audio books to increase the number of books they consume, without overwhelming them. Consider using an Amazon Kindle Paperwhite e-reader, which will mask the size of the book from your child and allow you to use a larger font, so it seems like an easier book. For active learners, find books with an active main character, so your child can relate to what they are reading.

For reluctant readers, focus on very short classic books when possible. There are many great literary works that are remarkably short. Consider reading aloud the first chapter, to get them started with the story and pronunciation of character names.

Crane, Stephen *The Red Badge of Courage* (146 pages, instead of *War and Peace*, 1024 pages)
The story of Henry Fleming, a teenager who enlists with the Union Army in the hopes of fulfilling his dreams of glory.

Dostoyevsky, Fyodor *The Gambler*
At a casino in Germany, a Russian family awaits news that a wealthy relative has died, but to their dismay, she arrives and begins gambling away their inheritance at an alarming rate. As fortunes are squandered and gained, lives are increasingly tied to the fickle rules of chance.

Hemingway, Ernest *Old Man and the Sea* (128 pages, instead of *Moby Dick*, 486 pages)
The exciting story of an old Cuban fisherman and his supreme ordeal: a relentless, agonizing battle with a giant marlin far out in the Gulf Stream.

London, Jack *Call of the Wild*
Set in Yukon Territory during the 19th-century Klondike Gold Rush, a domesticated dog is snatched and sold into a brutal life as a sled dog, where he struggles to survive.

Melville, Herman *Billy Budd* (instead of *Moby Dick*)
The story of an innocent young man unable to defend himself against a wrongful accusation.

Shelley, Mary *Frankenstein*
Frankenstein is a young man fascinated by science and attempts to unlock the secrets of life and death.

Steinbeck, John *Of Mice and Men*
In Depression-era California, two migrant workers dream of better days on a spread of their own, until an act of unintentional violence leads to tragic consequences.

Steinbeck, John *The Pearl*
A young, strong, and poor Mexican-Indian pearl diver must find a way to pay the town doctor to cure his son. Then he discovers an enormous pearl the size of a seagull's egg when out diving.

Kinesthetic learners

Focus on books with active main characters. Again, short books may be helpful, but it's even more important to choose active main characters, rather than primarily pensive characters. Here are just a few examples.

London, Jack *Call of the Wild*
In the extreme conditions of the Yukon during the 19th-century Klondike Gold Rush, a domesticated dog is snatched and sold into a brutal life as a sled dog,

where he struggles to adjust and survive the cruel treatment he receives from humans, other dogs, and nature.

Twain, Mark *The Adventures of Tom Sawyer*
A humorous and nostalgic book depicting the carefree days of boyhood in a small Midwestern town during the mid-1800s.

Twain, Mark *The Adventures of Huckleberry Finn*
The young Huck Finn flees with his old friend Jim, and they journey down the Mississippi River.

Prolific Readers

Voracious readers can sometimes use encouragement to feed their book hunger with quality literature rather than junk. If you have a literary lover at your house, you can increase their intake of great books by simply offering "collections" rather than individual books. Here are some examples that my prolific reader loved:

Austen, Jane *Jane Austen Four Novels*
Four of her best-loved novels: *Sense and Sensibility*, *Pride and Prejudice*, *Emma*, and *Northanger Abbey*

Tolkien, J. R. R. *J.R.R. Tolkien Boxed Set (The Hobbit and The Lord of the Rings)*
Four novels: *The Hobbit, The Fellowship of the Ring, The Two Towers, The Return of the King*

Dickens, Charles *Major Works of Charles Dickens* (Penguin Classics set)
Great Expectations, Hard Times, Oliver Twist, A Christmas Carol, Bleak House, A Tale of Two Cities

Popular Literature

A variety of colleges have said that homeschool applicants may have an over-emphasis on classic literature, and that reading lists should include popular literature. Some colleges have mentioned that inclusion of current literature shows "socialization." You may want to include some popular fiction in your student's reading list. For example, this recent book has become a modern classic.

Stockett, Kathryn *The Help*
The story of black maids raising white children in Mississippi during the 1960s civil rights movement.

Word of Caution

All families are different, and therefore all families must decide their own standards for the books their children read. Some of these books are listed on almost every reading list, but that doesn't mean they are perfect for you. This reading list is drawn from a broad cross section of college-bound reading lists. However, parents assume all responsibility for their children's education. If you are not familiar with something on this list, please review the book first.

You can find a printable reading list at: homehighschoolhelp.com/pdf/College-Bound-Reading-List.pdf

Afterword

Who is Lee Binz, and What Can She Do for Me?

Number one best-selling homeschool author, Lee Binz is The HomeScholar. Her mission is "helping parents homeschool high school." Lee and her husband, Matt, homeschooled their two boys, Kevin and Alex, from elementary through high school.

Upon graduation, both boys received four-year, full tuition scholarships from their first choice university. This enables Lee to pursue her dream job—helping parents homeschool their children through high school.

On The HomeScholar website, you will find great products for creating homeschool transcripts and comprehensive records to help you amaze and impress colleges.

Find out why Andrew Pudewa, Founder of the Institute for Excellence in Writing says, "Lee Binz knows how to navigate this often confusing and frustrating labyrinth better than anyone."

You can find Lee online at:

HomeHighSchoolHelp.com

If this book has been helpful, could you please take a minute to write us a quick review on Amazon?

Thank you!

Testimonials

I wanted to present Nate's accomplishments in the best possible light, **and I believe the course descriptions and small portfolio of work does a wonderful job of capturing what he accomplished** in home school. I would NEVER have gotten this far without you... I probably would have given up or done something simple and not adequately reflective of Nate's high school. So, the application materials are in the mail on their way to University!

~ Ann in Connecticut

We dropped Britt off at Northwest University Wednesday. During the registration process, one of the check in staff stopped me and said, *'Your documents for Britt when applying to NU were amazing. We would like to use them as a model for others, as they were really helpful for us and especially for homeschoolers!'*

Of course, I followed the Comprehensive Record Solution that you provided, and heard about your success with the admission process...but never expected to hear it for our own admission for Britt! I believe that his homeschool accomplishments, along with his comprehensive record, enabled us to set him up for an amazing start to his first year of college.

After auditioning for a talent scholarship, he was chosen to be the pianist for the Northwest Choralons, and received 50% more above the max for the talent scholarship to NU. We used many of the things you modeled in the Comprehensive Record Solution to create a music resume we submitted to each college.

Thank you AGAIN for a wonderful resource, and the training you provide to help us along the way.

~Lisa

Also From The HomeScholar...

- The HomeScholar Guide to College Admission and Scholarships: Homeschool Secrets to Getting Ready, Getting In and Getting Paid (Print and Kindle Book)
- Setting the Records Straight—How to Craft Homeschool Transcripts and Course Descriptions for College Admission and Scholarships (Print and Kindle Book)
- TechnoLogic: How to Set Logical Technology Boundaries and Stop the Zombie Apocalypse (Print and Kindle Book)
- Finding the Faith to Homeschool High School (Print and Kindle Book)
- The Easy Truth About Homeschool Transcripts (Kindle Book)

- Parent Training A la Carte (Online Training)
- Total Transcript Solution (Online Training, Tools and Templates)
- Comprehensive Record Solution (Online Training, Tools and Templates)
- Gold Care Club (Comprehensive Online Support and Training)
- Silver Training Club (Online Training)

The HomeScholar Coffee Break Books Released or Coming Soon on Kindle and Paperback:

- Delight Directed Learning: Guiding Your Homeschooler Toward Passionate Learning
- Creating Transcripts for Your Unique Child: Help Your Homeschool Graduate Stand Out from the Crowd
- Beyond Academics: Preparation for College and for Life
- Planning High School Courses: Charting the Course Toward High School Graduation
- Graduate Your Homeschooler in Style: Make Your Homeschool Graduation Memorable

- Keys to High School Success: Get Your Homeschool High School Started Right!
- Getting the Most Out of Your Homeschool This Summer: Learning just for the Fun of it!
- Finding a College: A Homeschooler's Guide to Finding a Perfect Fit
- College Scholarships for High School Credit: Learn and Earn With This Two-for-One Strategy!
- College Admission Policies Demystified: Understanding Homeschool Requirements for Getting In
- A Higher Calling: Homeschooling High School for Harried Husbands (by Matt Binz, Mr. HomeScholar)
- Gifted Education Strategies for Every Child: Homeschool Secrets for Success
- College Application Essays: A Primer for Parents
- Creating Homeschool Balance: Find Harmony Between Type A and Type Zzz...
- Homeschooling the Holidays: Sanity Saving Strategies and Gift Giving Ideas
- Your Goals this Year: A Year by Year Guide to Homeschooling High School

- Making the Grades: A Grouch-Free Guide to Homeschool Grading
- High School Testing: Knowledge That Saves Money
- Getting the BIG Scholarships: Learn Expert Secrets for Winning College Cash!
- Easy English for Simple Homeschooling: How to Teach, Assess and Document High School English
- Scheduling—The Secret to Homeschool Sanity: Plan You Way Back to Mental Health
- Junior Year is the Key to High School Success: How to Unlock the Gate to Graduation and Beyond
- Upper Echelon Education: How to Gain Admission to Elite Universities
- How to Homeschool College: Save Time, Reduce Stress and Eliminate Debt
- Homeschool Curriculum That's Effective and Fun: Avoid the Crummy Curriculum Hall of Shame!
- Comprehensive Homeschool Records: Put Your Best Foot Forward to Win College Admission and Scholarships
- Options After High School: Steps to Success for College or Career

- How to Homeschool 9th and 10th Grade: Simple Steps for Starting Strong!
- Senior Year Step-by-Step: Simple Instructions for Busy Homeschool Parents
- How to Homeschool Independently: Do-it-Yourself Secrets to Rekindle the Love of Learning
- High School Math The Easy Way: Simple Strategies for Homeschool Parents in Over Their Heads
- Homeschooling Middle School with Powerful Purpose: How to Successfully Navigate 6th through 8th Grade
- Simple Science for Homeschooling High School: Because Teaching Science isn't Rocket Science!

Would you like to be notified when we offer the next *Coffee Break Books* for FREE during our Kindle promotion days? If so, leave your name and email below and we will send you a reminder.

HomeHighSchoolHelp.com/freekindlebook

Visit my Amazon Author Page!
amazon.com/author/leebinz